The Fox jumps over the Parson's Gate

Randolph Caldecott

[ZHINGOORA BOOKS]

THE FOX JUMPS OVER THE PARSON'S GATE

The Huntsman blows his horn in the morn,

When folks goes hunting, oh!

When folks goes hunting, oh!

When folks goes hunting, oh!

The Huntsman blows his horn in the morn,

When folks goes hunting, oh!

The Fox jumps over the Parson's gate,

And the Hounds all after him go,

And the Hounds all after him go,

And the Hounds all after him go.

But all my fancy dwells on Nancy,

So I'll cry, Tally-ho!

So I'll cry, Tally-ho!

Now the Parson had a pair to wed

As the Hounds came full in view;

He tossed his surplice over his head,

And bid them all adieu!

But all my fancy dwelt on Nancy,

So he cried, Tally-ho!

So he cried, Tally-ho!

Oh! never despise the soldier-lad

Though his station be but low,

Though his station be but low,

Though his station be but low.

But all my fancy dwells on Nancy,

So I'll cry, Tally-ho!

Then pass around the can, my boys;

For we must homewards go,

For we must homewards go,

For we must homewards go.

And if you ask me of this song

The reason for to shew,

I don't exactly know-ow-ow

I don't exactly know

But all my fancy dwells on Nancy,

So I'll sing, Tally-ho!

So I'll sing, Tally-ho!

But all my fancy dwells on Nancy,

So I'll sing, TALLY-HO!

The End

www.ingramcontent.com/pod-product-compliance
Lightning Source LLC
Chambersburg PA
CBHW070123010626
45794CB00012B/1278